NEEDLE IN THE EYE

NEEDLE IN THE EYE

POEMS NEW AND OLD

R.A.D. FORD

MOSAIC PRESS

Canadian Cataloguing in Publication Data

Ford, R. A. D., 1915-
    Needle in the eye

ISBN 0-88962-220-5 (bound). - ISBN 0-88962-219-1 (pbk.)

I. Title.

PS8511.O72N43 1983   C811'.54   C83-099045-3
PR9199.3.F66N43 1983

Published by Mosaic Press, P.O. Box 1032, Oakville, Ontario, L6J 5E9, Canada.

Published with the assistance of the Canada Council and the Ontario Arts Council.

Copyright © R.A.D. Ford, 1983.
Cover drawing by Michel Chemiakine
Typeset by Speed River Graphics.
Design by Doug Frank.
Printed and bound by Les Editions Marquis Ltee, Montmagny, Quebec.
Printed and bound in Canada.

ISBN 0-88962-220-5 cloth
ISBN 0-88962-219-1 paper

Distributed in the United States by Flatiron Books, 175 Fifth Avenue, Suite 814, New York, N.Y. 10010, U.S.A.

Distributed in the U.K. by John Calder (Publishers) Ltd., 18 Brewer Street, London W1R 4AS, England.

Distributed in New Zealand and Australia by Pilgrims South Press, P.O. Box 5101, Dunedin, New Zealand.

Simply,
for
Thereza

Other Books by R.A.D. Ford

A Window on the North (1956)
The Solitary City (1969)
Holes in Space (1979)

The older poems are reproduced with the permission of the successors to the Ryerson Press, Toronto: *A Window on the North* 1956; McClelland and Stewart, Toronto: *The Solitary City* 1969; and the Hounslow Press, Toronto: *Holes in Space* 1979.

Some of the new poems have appeared in The Malahat Review; Prism International; Poetry Canada Review; Canadian Literature, and the Anthology of Magazine Verse and American Poetry 1981 Edition.

CONTENTS

THE WORLD OF R.A.D. FORD

In this our world of very little grace and of very few who miss the absence, the attestation to the contrary of Robert Ford is an act that goes directly to the welcoming heart and an act that is in itself an embodiment of grace. The man believes in the efficacy of love and the man who is the poet believes that the efficacy of love is identical with the grace with which the poem is made. Nothing adequately warns us, he tells us, of the destructiveness of our times except an act of love. Cruelty is posted everywhere, nothing

> Runs before the earthquake to say
> That the streets are opening, the fire
> Prepared and the waters of the bay
> Ready to resume their empire,

nothing save the woman running with a cry of warning before the earthquake with her "testimony of love."

That her warning may be too late does not minimize the efficacy of love. Without love,

> the universe
> Settles into its usual disarray.

Robert Ford should know. He does know. For how many years has he been at the heart of things governmental and political? Ever since 1940, his purview taking in more than half the world, an ambassador not only to those thousands of miles swung around the pivot of political Ottawa but a knowing observer posted at those places on the globe most likely to be the epicentre of the metaphorical earthquake: South America, Eastern Europe, the Middle East, Moscow.

What it means to have a poet thus placed at the troubled centres of human affairs is to have experience interpreted by human considerations, not politics, not diplomacy, not postures, but by the truths of the heart by which we all live, by which we wish to live; it is to have these truths, won by circumstance and destiny, find expression in forms of lasting worth. For truth is best served by poetry. A poem which lies is a bad poem; it is discarded, it won't do. Truth only will do, since a poem must have a verbal grace and since all words carry meaning, wrongness given to the meaning destroys the essential grace.

Poets listened-to would better the world. Shelley in this is right; Auden who tells us that poetry makes nothing happen is wrong. Poetry refreshes the heart. It cannot wind clocks but it tells the time. The world does not listen to truth-tellers — except perhaps a century too late. Robert Ford tells us. So all poets tell us. But we have the truth and we have our nostalgia when we read poets too late. Such as that is. Perhaps the residue of regret works on the contemporary heart. Who proves otherwise?

11

Robert Ford is at present on the Palme Disarmament Commission; he is, though retired from his ambassadorships in the official world, Special Advisor on East-West Relations to our government in Ottawa. It refreshes the heart to know this. A poet at the centre of affairs? How can human matters be forwarded therefore but by humanity? Chaucer was worth sixteen pound sterling to the government who ransomed him from abroad. A price madly at variance to the value of having a poetic imagination qualifying our worldly doings, the sensation of daylight regained. Not that a poet cannot be up to mischief, be a scoundrel perhaps, but only for himself, the poetry is never at the expense of someone else. It must so go against the grain with the poet as ambassador when he must follow the duplicity of his government, that he cannot write. Or write well — despite the example of Dryden.

Of official commendation of Robert Ford there is evidence from everywhere he has been. England, Brazil, Colombia, Yugoslavia, Egypt, the Sudan, Mongolia and Russia. "An extraordinary Canadian, a distinguished personality, a remarkable representative of his country. You don't expect to have more than one or two men like him in his generation," thus runs the commendation. Robert Ford is a Companion of the Order of Canada.

Here, we have him, in this book, non-officially. The vast experience of life and the private sensitivity are here, as they should be, in splendid retrospect and in their forecasting of the poems still to come from him. "I have travelled," says Ford, "in pretty weird places — the Mato Grosso of the Brazilian interior; Bolivia's uplands; the Maddalena Valley in Colombia; all over the Sudan; China, India and the Middle East; and of course the whole of the USSR, including Siberia a couple of times." There is little experience of the world that Ford cannot provide. His first book, A Window on the North, winner of the Governor General's Award for poetry in 1956, gave us what the title indicates, but a window too on the world as looked through by other poets. A fluent possessor of languages other than English, wherever that window was provided Ford has translated for us what other poets have seen. He has, to use phrases of his own, "let down the political barriers" and "surmounted the obstacle of language". He has done this memorably in translations and adaptations of modern Brazilian poetry, Serbo-Croatian, superbly of Russian poets of the century. I remember looking at the translations of Pasternak's poems that accompanied the western appearance of Pasternak's novel "Dr. Zhivago" and then reading Ford's translations — the latter far superior: they were good English poems.

I repeat here the delightful story that Time magazine told of Robert Ford attending the United Nations Assembly's first meeting in London in 1946. "There, one engaging day, he listened with amusement as a pretty young Brazilian delegate gossiped aloud, in Portuguese, about the other delegates. Leaning down from his 6 ft. 3 in., Ford quietly informed her: 'It's about time you Brazilians realized that Portuguese is not a secret language.' They were married a few weeks later." The pretty delegate was Thereza Gomes from Rio de Janeiro. I had met Thereza even before — any litterateur could guess where: in New York at Frances Steloff's Gotham Book Mart on West 47th Street, the mecca of international writers. Later, in New York, with my wife, the four of us dined; still later the four of us dined in Moscow. How much of the vitality of Robert's poetry is Thereza? It must be a formidable quantity. The vivacity! I suppose the limousine was under eavesdropped surveillance when Thereza, on our way to the Bolshoi Theatre in Moscow (Robert was absent), denounced refreshingly loudly the adulation that could put up a bronze statue to the head of the KGB as we passed it; and seated in the refreshment room of the Bolshoi could likewise refreshingly describe in more than single-table hearing what the true quality of the ballet champagne was. Little wonder Robert's poetry has gone on inspiredly.

That window on the north which Robert Ford has is more than Akhenaten's "Window of Appearances." His is a window on truth. Ford derives from Ottawa and London, Ontario. Somewhat in his poems of the Canadian north we hear the note which Duncan Campbell Scott struck. An odd reverberation — because Ford is of his own time in form and technique — but there nevertheless in that tone of northness; more outwardly tragic than Lampman was in that scene; more cosmopolitan (in the right, non-superficial sense) than Duncan Campbell Scott. But there it is: that northern sadness of Scott's half-breed girl and Ford's woman watching that north out her window at "Twenty Below":

> The woman goes to the window and presses her hand
> against the glacial pane, and leans her head
> against the frame. Her breath has made a hole
> in the frost. She can see outside the northern cold
> smothering the world...

and the woman
>   takes her sadness
>   and thaws it before the flames.

That is an early poem. But the distinction of Ford's poetry is that there is nothing in Ford's work of that garrison attitude that accepts "twenty below" as being the terrible constant of all Canada huddling its

13

barricades. Ford is too mature for that. The legend of the wolf is there, the monster of the north, "impervious / To the settler's gun." It is a north that Russia has, as the skies of Canada are the skies of Scandinavia; there is always

> The entrance unperceived
> Of the cold season.

But it is not the cold geography beloved by Canadians because, so the critics tell us, Canadians love being victims. Ford's geography is emancipated; there is no Canadian monopoly on survival and victimization; Ford breaks the bonds of locality:

> My feet squelch in the mud
> And up through the soles
> Comes the feel of the underworld.

If the mood is still of loneliness, vastness, melancholy, what poet of contemporary sensitivity can write otherwise? There is love. There is always the world against it.

It is this profoundly simple knowledge that Ford writes about — this opposition, this counterpoint, this confrontation. Perhaps too much so. But here again is this man's distinguished experience. But note well, there is still behind the disillusionment that affirmative measurement without which there would be no disillusionment. Call it love. If, like "the lame, the halt, the twisted" we are unwhole

> And into the solitary city,
> Turning again,

> Pull down the blinds
> On solitary streets,

it is because we "deny / The core of love."

> The white
> Geometry of winter leaves no margin
> For error, no relic in the snow.

Accuracy is preferable. The half-perfect of Alexandria is preferred to the perfection of Greece-alas, "Wrenched / From history."
Better to plunge

> into the barren
> Truth at the dead centre.

With a sort of lowering of style, simply because he has achieved a style, Robert Ford writes on, from his second book, *The Solitary City*, to his third, *Holes in Space*, a book of achieved lucidity and of almost fatalistic non-innocence, a book of moving, dark lyricism of a maturity of years where

> The colours of the autumn hill

14

Seem more important than
Decisions for tomorrow,
And the preservation of the rose
To the deadly fate of man.

There is "the hubbub of April" to deal with,

the tendrils of love
Thrust up through the pavement.

The clangour of time
Bursts out and overwhelms
The lies, walls, webs, the last
Snow flakes, ash, dust, dirt,
The gravel of deceit.

Affirmation is in triumph. As all disillusioned poets of worth declare,
the world is to be loved. Robert Ford knows that the answer is love.

The message I get is blurred
Except for the cypher of your smile.

He has broken the code.

Perverse I am, persistant
In error. But the world is bright
There is no sour image,
No general disarray.

And so, with fingers crossed,
I put aside my gloom,
Grasp the happy dawn,
And quietly disengage.

—Ralph Gustafson

A NOTE

This collection contains some twenty new poems and a selection from my previous volumes of verse. I have arranged the previously published poems in rough chronological order. They treat primarily the themes of philosophy, love, nature, particularly that of Canada, politics, and my experiences of other countries and other cultures.

The long poem, *Luis Medias Pontual in Red Square*, is based on the experiences of a refugee from the Spanish Civil War, many of whom fled to the USSR in 1939, and practically all of whom found the land and the system intolerable. In his words I have tried to express the disgust and disillusionment of so many people with the Soviet Union when, after the War, Stalin quickly shed the mask he had worn during the conflict and reverted to the more primeval and repulsive features of Stalinism in action.

R.A.D. FORD

PART I — POEMS NEW

SLEEPLESSNESS OF OUR TIME

This is a decade of insomnia
The nights white with fear
Every dawn is a sigh every day
Seems to greet another year

If in the dark you lift your hand
Or move the counter-pane
I know you wait with choked breath
As I do for the rain

Or for a wind to stir the leaves
Or touch the window-sill
And all the ghosts detach themselves
From the corners of the hall

And when we do sleep brokenly
With dusk in our eyes
We are afraid of suddenly speaking
The truth in any guise

Every day is a year gained
And two lost every night
The wonder is we do not fall
Faster out of sight

Maybe there is a pill to take
Against this century
But I think our conscience is too bad
For any remedy

1979

RECOLLECTING

In frozen forests of memory
Rain falls like unparsed verbs,
And the decyphering of the words
Is a task beyond reality.

Freezing as it falls to a kind
Of shimmering sleet,
The rain transforms the trees
And the forest becomes fantasy.

The clue is not in the words
Or in the unreal woods.
I have it in my hands
And a recollected look.

I imprisoned it before
You could stop the flight
Of talk. I hear the whir of wings
As the words flee into night.

1981

HAPPY QUIETUDE
"Tout à coup on se sent touché"

— Henri Michaux

Suddenly the door shuts
Absolutely, the shutters
Swing to; the fantasies
Of silence slip up the wall,
While a wisp of wind chatters.

Suddenly I am full
Of awareness, a happy
Quietude; you have not
Touched me, you are not there,
Your perfume is a copy.

But inside the shuttered room
Your hand is in mine,
And the many years of distance
Contract with time.

1980

VATICINATION

The inventory of my dreams
Is incomplete, and these words
Are used to weave
A strange to-morrow.

Slowly the text closes round us.
But, peering into a dimly
Perceived future, I can
Traverse the transparent

Distance between us,
Bringing words of love
Which have the look
Of menhirs.

1982

POEM

The time has come to conjugate
    with the transitive verb.
If we wish to escape with a small
    dose of irresponsibility.
Who does not love it, seeking to
    walk in pre-history?
Discipline is limited to
    a few basic facts.
And the choices to be made are
    simple and instinctive.

1980

THE MONGOLS

I look towards Astrakhan across the lean
Gray Volga steppe, dusted lightly
With dirty snow. That anonymous space

Of Russia was its saviour before
The ponies of Batu the Terrible swiftly
Destroyed distance and time in the Blitzkrieg

Of the East. They shouted in the streets
Of the ravaged cities: 'Regret
Is the fruit of pity". And the savage

Warriors impressed their stain
On the Russian soil. Our eyes, blinded
By the glare of history, strain

Past the huts and the golden domes
To the centre of the world.
No voyager has ever told its mystery,

What the vortex of the globe has held.
No man fathomed the Golden Horde;
Who is the scourge of Europe? Who tolls

The bell? What force released those arms
Of hate? And what survived? What still
Lives on in other forms?
And who pronounced the word to kill.

1980

LOVE POEM

When first I captured through despair
The abstract meaning of your smile,
I thought I'd happened on a seer,

Or fallen on a guide to share
The mystery of the final mile,
And look beyond the distant shore.

You fashioned theorems out of air,
You let intelligence beguile
The many who admired your fair

Face, your mind alert, your care
For beauty, for the mind, the while
You sought wide-eyed the lesser cure

To go on living. And it was there
We crossed. The world began to feel
Coherent, and the truant fear

Of childhood's dark and threatening stair
Dissolved. The magic turned into the real,
And the real turned magically clear.

1982

EXCESS OF NIGHT

Winter in Ungava turns the hard
Man into a blind guide in the excess
Of night. But the Eskimo sees easily
With the twenty-seven colours of snow.

I am at a loss in my strange world.
I stumble in the dark. I have only
A drop of water, a few words on my tongue.
And when I meet some-one, those words

Are incomprehensible in the language
Of solitude. We share the same
Latitude, but no words traverse
The pole, not even cross

The brief distance that separates
Them from us, you from me.
The space around us has the shape
Of silence, and I cannot grasp

The size or feel of it, or what it means.
But silence is an adequate cure
When nothing can be done but wait
For the smothering northern night to end.

1980

A WONDROUS SUMMER

Into the veined grape the light
Of morning sought eternal joy,
The dream of fruit and bough.

It was mingled with the sight
Of your early morning face,
And the sunshine on your brow.

It was summer like forever,
Days that never died, night
White, fleeting like a dawn.

Only a distant tremour
Left memory disavowed,
And the future placed in pawn.

Only a shade across the sun
Sent less than eternity
Into that wondrous day.

But we were not aware the sun
Was less than perfect nor that
The summer would not stay.

We only saw translucent,
In our unique and northern land,
Light on the grape and veined leaves,
And the promise held in your hand.

1980

NEEDLE IN THE EYE

For Henri Michaux

The logic of our times
Breaks like a thread, and my
Fingers are not firm enough
To bring it back again through
The eye of the needle.

It is the reverse. The needle
Is in my eye, and I am blind
By day, and at night navigate
Alone in a scorched country-side.

I walk surrounded
By silent agony. It is not
My pain, but the lonely eyes
That follow me in their dead holes,

The craters in the tundra
Of our century, the faint query
In the night sky that haunts
The questioning man,

A voice thrown into the middle
Of winter, the water which
Escapes between our porous
Fingers, our decade's rationale.

The needle was never there.
In the abstruse logomachy
Of our time it never was, and
The broken logic as improbable

As infallability. Only, now
I am one with the solitary
Wanderers in the wood,
Taking one careful step at a time.

1982

THE AGE OF TERRORISM

Trying to avoid the land mines
I walk dangerously close to the edge
Of our time, not looking at the drop
Vertiginous, out of sight, out of mind.

I was warned the mines were laid
Haphazardly, the symbol of our age.
The violence that we spurn and love
Is the dreadful renegade.

Obsesses all of us, not me alone,
The blood, the blow, the sudden hit.
Love perhaps I can bring with me
To face the chill unknown.

Love must be the only help,
A half choice in the soaring void,
As we walk the path between the mines,
Towards a universe destroyed.

1979

OPTICAL ILLUSION

The times take me by the throat,
Like a pathetic strangler
Without the force to kill,

Wanting yet unwilling, unable
To press the fingers of argument
Through the jugular.

But I suffocate all the same.
It Is the facility that alarms.
The theme barely passes

From page to page, from day
To reluctant day. Teletype
To the moon, satellite

To the Middle Kingdom. And
Back to me in a country beyond
Geography, where the hours

Are immobilised, and the clocks
Silently mark the internal
Passage of a stray thought.

The hands of the smog slacken,
My eyes return to their sockets,
True shapes of history appear.

The dispatches are solid with
Ascertainable facts. And, after all,
The world is not coming to an end.

1980

TRUCE

"Le coeur, comme des rois, sous la forme de paix perpétuelle,
ne signe donc que les trêves " — Amiel

The war goes on, the words wound
Murderously, the blood flows and quickens,
Until the sacrifice is too great
And the heart sickens.

The emissaries sound out the enemy,
Cease-fire is called, the barrage dies down,
The sky is seen again through the haze
and recognizable is the dawn.

Peace for a century should be ours,
But the heart opts only for a truce,
Though there is time enough for a hand-clasp
In the ruins of those countless Troys.

We think it is the threshold,
The going in, the promise, the rosy
Future. But the armistice
Is like the wraith of a passing thought,
And our hearts harden with the sight of peace.

1981

POLITICAL SCIENCE

There is a hunger in the heart,
Tasting of salt on desert stone,
There is thirst unappeased,
And a planet's sudden shadow.

In this hour of stridency,
This hard and dangerous time
Spawns distorted virtues
Out of vices half-forgot.

The earth seems shudderingly
To shift as the axis turns.
The fault line is real,
And the continents begin

To drift back into each
Other's arms through the gulf
Of the diminishing sea.
Our thoughts across the spheres

Seem sucked into vacuum,
And no compatible idea
Comes through with clarity.
We have a fault line all

Our own, and the experts confidently
Predict catastrophe.
But no true seismist knows
When the continents will close.

1982

GESTURES

My only gesture is a symbol,
My regard a reflection of the simple
Truth, and the mirror becomes
A pool of indifference.

The glassy surface is like
The facades of buildings which
No longer coincide with the line
Of the street or the design

Of the long-dead architect.
Finding the entrance must be
Tied to a code, or sought
In exotic documents.

Gestures are the symbolism
Of the past. They strike a chord
Of sympathy in ancient
History. They have no place

In our own peculiar age.
They reflect the treachery of glass,
The vacuity of words,
The emptiness of promise.

1980

A WORD OF COURAGE

The months trail in the slime of winter,
And I agonize in the slum of March.
Foot-steps drag in the slush and mud.
My spirit leaves me in the lurch.

Till a sudden lift in the ragged clouds
Brings spring with a rush into my blood,
Like a word of courage from the camps
For us poor weaklings under God.

1980

OLD GEOGRAPHY

In the humourless geography
Of a young continent, we look
For a novel vegetation
In the fog-drenched valleys;

From a new world star trek
Search out a formula for
Acceptance, not ghostly foot-steps
Upwards in the jargon of space;

From our familiar shore discover
No philosophy to hide
The barrenness of the desert land
Already in our suburbs.

1980

THE SEEPAGE OF WILL

There is a seepage of will
In all of us. I prefer
The ephemeral to the real.
The colours of the autumn

Seem more important than
Decisions for tomorrow,
And the preservation of the rose
To the deadly fate of man.

Dark clouds line up across
The horizon, with a smell
Of winter in the air. The time
Has come to close

The book but the poetry
Like smoke invades the will.
And the water seeps out
Leaving a dry well.

1982

TIME LIKE A WEED

I have watched time grow
Like weeds in a rain-forest,
And have barely noted
That November has dusted
The woods with frost.

Looking through the window
I see dreams frozen to the pane,
A hand outspread;
And beyond the scarcely
Visible trees, the falling sky.

I can leave at any time,
Unencumbered, and venture
Into the winter woods.

1981

SIBERIA

This northern wound laid bare
To the unpractised urgent hand
Cries in the crystal night
To the heart and the bludgeoned head.

Salt in the open veins,
Terror in the dusk, the dead,
The dead with open eyes,
Under the frozen pines.

1979

THE COAST OF CHILDHOOD

The coast of childhood looms close,
And there is a sudden pinching
Of the muscles below the heart —
Either a premonition of the end,
Or a spilling-over of regret.

And suddenly I have a desperate need
To know the books which define us,
To pursue the contours of the past,
To seize the inevitability
Of decay in our precarious age.

I want to walk back into time
With the clear eye of understanding,
And to search on those distant shores
For the word lost long ago, knowing
It is not there and never was.

1982

PART II — POEMS OLD
1940-1950

TWENTY BELOW

The woman watches her husband rubbing his nose,
frozen while chopping a hole in the river's ice,
now thawing slowly between his hands and snow —
sitting by the stove with his peasant eyes nowhere
and his feet in their ribbed grey homespun stockings placed
in the oven, the fire roaring with the top grate raised,
the pipes and flues across the room near white
with heat. The mongrel restless at his side
creeps closer to the fire. The children doze,
half living only through the frozen days.
The woman goes to the window and presses her hand
against the glacial pane, and leans her head
against the frame. Her breath has made a hole
in the frost. She can see outside the northern cold
smothering the world; and an impossible sleep
and silence falling from a sky of slate,
even the pines grey and rigid and still,
the mighty hills mere shadows on the pale
immeasurable horizon.

Without reason,
feeling only her heart oppressive within her
and her life stopped dead and motionless in the
hoar
and drifted week, she weeps, and the tears
become
cold rivulets that cut across her cheeks.

                    The cold presses into the room
from every side through the logs and stones and chinks
between the logs, so the circle of people sinks
into sopor, and the woman takes her sadness
and thaws it before the flames.

1940

45

LYNX

Consignee of silent storms and unseen lightning,
soft violence, oppresor of new fallen snow,
moving like the winter solstice through
the beautiful woods, none so
lovely even in eyes yellow in white
fur the betrayer; the leap without
muscle swelling, small cloud blotting
out the bright day — Will not languish
in the cruel trap, the cruel eyes
and cruel claws wounded, the hunters shouting
in victory, gloating at the anguish
in the mighty legs broken —
Will not linger broken but pass
suddenly with great pain into the Indian night.

1941

WOLF

Of danger to the innocent simpleton, no
Pity expressed because none wanted,
Hovering in the grip of cold unfelt
On the outskirts of the city, hunted
By hunger from the Arctic snow
To the warmth of the relative south,
Bursting all fang and steel from the field
Of winter on the wayward child.

And then the vicious chase to the woods,
Bounty tacked to a slavering mouth,
The dogs floundering in the drifts, wild
With fear and bravado. But gone
Shadow, again and again, struck down
In the night till the April floods
Break boundaries of the frozen town.

The children look for flowers at
The forest edge, whispering with
Huge eyes and faces drawn
In terror of the grey shape behind
Each tree, at the rustle of brush
Flying to the meadow and voices
In the sun.

No-one ever saw him,
But more real to child the myth
In every game and tale, the hush
Of mystery and fear would fall,
The monster from the north, the grim
Siberian hate, than all known terrors
Of the street or book, impervious
To the settler's gun.

1941

A WINDOW ON THE NORTH

Stirb und werde — Goethe

The whole landscape drifted away to the north,
To Moose Factory, hundreds of miles, to the pole
And beyond, to the Arctic ends of the earth,
Sullen, Siberian, grey, only the hills and
Humps of snow, and the frightening black
Of the evergreens before us. The window
Was white with frost, inviting and beckoning the
Famishing cold into the room, into the very heart,
Into our true sadness, the gripping melancholy.

We drowsed with the languor of the battling
Heat from the ugly stove and the cramping
Weariness. Three jays lay dead,' their toes
Frozen to the icy juniper boughs, their blue
Plumage arranged artistically on the bush.
The uranium and gold capered like heroes
In a Chaplin film, and the Hollywood Indian
Rocked in the hush and dreamed of York boats
Down the Saskatchewan.

                    Die and become.
Die and become, Johnny Cree, the standing warrior.
Die and become in this vast waste of yours —
A blue-jay to come again in the sudden
Summer, now so lovely dead, a white fox
Out of the tundra, a mere thought over
The snow — warrior and wanderer once more
In the barrens of the world.

                    A geranium plant
Stood on a shelf behind him. Putney in extremis.
Suddenly it was all red with flower,
Glowing with magic, defiant to the great
White bear. I thought of you in the sweet
South; and the wind at the window was only
A warm breeze to melt the icicles of sleep.

1942

REVENGE OF THE HUNTED

The gun, the trap, the axe are borne
head high at dusk in triumph home —
the tramp of hunting boots,
the bloody mantle thrown
down, these challenge to the soul
the flagrant horn, and send
to the far bounds of the green
hills the trumpeting of death in shame.

There will be a beating out some day,
from bush to field to stone
farm; then, lugged in the mud,
spattered with wings torn and unclean
ugly parts of snake and lame
beasts, will with crude
arms barbarously destroy,
with fierce voices savagely proclaim:
Here lies the broken gun alone,
the green weeds sweeping it away,
and here the judgement of the wood.

1943

ROADSIDE NEAR MOSCOW

Bent and heavy with rain,
Staggering in silence, profoundly
Occupied with the secret reconstruction
Of their balance, pine and tamarack
Trees, gathered in profane

Assembly to watch over the slow
Passing of the almost human-like
Column of prisoners, waiting for the snow
To fill in their tracks — strange
Judges of evil done

In many ways. Because I am not
Walking in chains, and am afraid
To look, lest by implication
Glance should be said guilty,
Unhappily turn my head

To the stale spectacle of the sun
Setting among the conifers.
And when it is gone, look down
For the column of men in vain —
In the thick arch of night

That has come suddenly,
Hobble my eyes to perceive
Nothing but the rain, turning
To snow, — all that I wish to see.

1947

BACK TO DUBLIN

From Drogheda all along the coast, the Irish Sea,
Followed by the ghost of the Marquis of I don't
Remember, but his car overwhelmed us with dust
Near Rush and his castle, a constant grey
Landmark all over Meath, appeared to say
Continually to us, second immigrants: what
Is the use of coming back to stare? While others, the poor
Relations, either jeered or seemed to think
We were there to gloat, had never heard
Of Joyce or Yeats, and glorified Thomas Moore,
Pointed out the shell marks in the Dublin streets,
And deferred the debate on the price of hogs
To show us where the Liffey meets with God.

No glory to come back, none to be there,
And none but the seer to tender why the pilgrimage
To the rain-washed isle; never got to the grave
Under Ben Bulben, nor Tara's Halls, nor Innisfree
In the heat of the year — but just to stand
Near the stained walls of the ancient town
And dream of sailing to Byzantium —
An old man and a damaged harp,
Weaving the sweetest pattern on the warp
Of a broken continent — that was my fee,
That was my ticket to come in.

1949

THE STICK LAID DOWN

The stick laid down, the club
dethroned, in the crushed wild
flowers tamed and soon
buried in the perfume now defiled
by barbarous feet led down
the valley in the wash of love,
recall the weapons used
in hate on the bare hills above.

And in the odorous bed, by
the side of the stick thrown
away, passes to love my
heart, my hate all gone,
the hills departed, left
decyphered in the maze
of leaves in the summer wind,
the code destroyed for the ways
of love; no shadow lies,
no mount of fear, no hill
to break the prairie of your eyes.

1950

LUIS MEDIAS PONTUAL IN RED SQUARE

Thousands of years stand before us like a cesspool. Inside the pool lie machines, bits, cast iron, tin, sinews, springs...A dark, gloomy pool. And fungus, mould. Our emotions! This is all that remains of our emotions, of the flowering of our souls. — Yuri Olesha [Envy]. 1927.

I

In the circle of your eyes the days
Repeat the cycle of our trial,
And now, not different from the hour
Of misery long past, the trail
More tortuous than it was,

We find the shuffle of our feet
On the fallen virgin snow
Is the slow movement to
Each world's end, from and to
The precipice and the fate

corny

Of man, and back to you
Who stop before the walls of God
To stare. The muffled noise
Of winter in the white street
Is almost silence in the cold

Expanse. Reluctantly our eyes
Look up from the brick red
Walls to the yellow palaces,
The souls of the long dead
Heroes, and our helpless gaze

For the hundredth time halt
At the glory of the domes,
Golden in the winter sun;
Forget the crows and jackdaws
Of harassed souls like old

Omens fluttering in the sky. Then
The hand of the militia-man on
Your arm: "Podi, podi" — Ancient
And universal as the phrase
Of all centuries enchained.

II

Rome is Rome no more.
The world has two eternal cities
Now: Madrid and Moscow.
We are the words of hate they use
To drive each other to the door

Of paradise. We are the winds
And seas of words that serve
Leviathan. I should like
To lie down in temperate shade,
Far from the city of my birth,

And the city of my exiled choice,
Out of the tyrannous sun,
And the oppressive snow,
To feel the soft hands of love
Silence the thinking lies,

Strip the lines from your brow
And the sadness from your eyes.
Not see you, now, your face
Rise pure from the vast
Anonymous, Eurasian mass,

Come strangely through the slow
Moving, silent, unbearable
Suffering of man, the crushing
Unsaved and unregenerate, terrible
Sorrow of those who

Said, this way is heaven
Found. And then again the surf
Of words sweep back across the steppe.
The sweet peace I wept
For is not for those who serve.

Oh Spain! I see you, Jerez
De la Frontera, in the breath
That stands up like statues
From our lips, like death
From the muzzle of a gun.

My tears are frozen in my eyes,
To throw them stones in
The street and let them roll
Home, my monument, is all
The sentiment I've still.

A tunnel of silence under the world
And my steps going down
To meet you! Meet you in the path
Of night, in the emptiness grown
Pure that needs no word.

III

Not the wind from Samarkand,
Not the wind from the Hungry Steppe,
Blew down the Iberian Virgin,
But the wild tempest from
The Finland Station.

Disappeared in the night and out
Of night was built the other shrine,
Black, red, solid, functional,
Factory for the Moscow soul,
The cenotaph of doubt.

Now I walk unhindered on the white
Emptiness of your shrine. Iberia!
Mystery of Spain lost in the heart
Of Russia, to whom interpreted
The exterior world a chart

For men in the passioned heat
Of Andalucia, or the Indies,
Or the seas of gold, but not the hate,
The fury of the Tartar wastes —
And we tread warily far

From the city of the gypsies where
I remember at my mother's side
The black and sculptured wood,
The tortured saints, were real
And present gods to fear.

And through those gates thrown wide
Forty civil guards surged in,
And rode to the sack through gods
I lost, through gods of blood,
Destroyed in youth

By Moorish guards and deaf
Priests, in prison camps and dead
Cities. Now you have come back
In the streets of refuge,

And angels walk before me,
Singing of the treasured skies
Of golden Andalucia; and the names
Of comrades of Guadalajara rise
Strangely from the snows.

IV

If there were each day a hill
That we could look upon and know
It would be there tomorrow, a tree
In the city where we could cry upon
Angels, and hear triumphantly

Their voices rejecting the charge
Of pavement, a shrine of mystery,
Gilded in the cement of hours
For working days, unpunctuated
By the strict, relentless dirge

Of factory whistles, time clocks —
A shadow even to hide
Two hands joined in love —
This hill, this tree, this shrine,
This shade, in the mind

Existing, were not made for flat
Statements in the grey squares of
Moscow; but in the remnants
Of the Mongol past, in the sad
Traces of the slum of the East,

Smelling of the just passage
Of Timor and Attila the Hun,
There in the black bright
Eyes of a Turkman sage,
There the mystery be found,
And there the ancient tree.

V

Russia and Spain, we suffered both
The blow of the Orient. This beggar
Mongol-eyed was once your
Conqueror and underneath his
Whip the Moscow princes bowed

Down before the Golden Horde —
In the ikon of Nereditsa portrayed
All the history of the Slavic pain
For a thousand years — in the ikon
Of Nereditsa all the swelling pain,

And sorrow and humanity of falling
Byzantium when the thundering Turk
Battered its inner walls transferred
To the wooden battlements of Russia,
Outpost of Christendom on the verge

Of the Asian flood — and the whole
Beauty of suffering and the urge
To martyrdom in the rough
Painting opposed to the arms
Of pitilessness. This is the last

Dreamer, an old Turkoman,
In rags, dirty, bearded,lost
In Russia, where once he broke
This Slavic mass of wondering
People as he breaks a crucifix
Across his knee, now dreaming

Of the strange force of the Rock
Of Athos that came to Novgorod, —
Lord of the quivering steppe, the last
Dreamer walked with faltering pace,
Eyes on the towers, hands clasped

In meditation to the fortress walls,
When a light flashed, bell rung,
The Kremlin gates flung wide
Released a cavalcade, and the sage
Went down beneath the wheels.

VI

With what syllables of love can I
Implore life to this ragged,
Useless soul? like Spain
Destroyed by fire from the aged
Furnaces of hate,

Not from within alone, not
Willingly rushing to sure
Death, but inevitably cast
Before the course of the four
Winds beating the flames

Ahead. Generations of snow
Will cover the body up. Years
Hence the ice will melt
And the smell from the new
And barren earth will rise

To the yellow walls. Turning
Their heads from the odour
Of centuries, we pass ignoring;
Nor can we seek for help

Forgetfulness or tears or dreams
Of Greece or Turkestan. In the ruts
Left black in the snow by trucks
And carts like pounding years,
The seed of Spring is green,

[One man can tell the names
Of God, and one is many yet.]
All the strange past cannot
Deny the boundaries of Russia
Which went to look for death

And searching not East or West
But underneath found God.
The seed I take from the snow,
A handful of dung, the flower
Of loneliness, a stone loaf, a rod

Of pity, the dust from the Iberian
Virgin's grave, the death that's
Not awaited, the white world!
The adoration and despair

Of Russia weigh upon me,
The wonder, the search, the foiled
Perfection, and the dead, the many dead.
Where have I failed,
And in what way, to understand?

Oh city of the gypsies, I can
Come back no more, but tell
The Civil Guard, the foe
Of simple men, I failed —
They will be glad to know.

1950

1951-1959

A DELUSION OF REFERENCE

The arms of the sea are extended,
The hills, which are not really mountains,
Extinguished, and a delusion
Of reference sets in when you spread
Your hair to the light. It is a contagion
Like any other, and in all the cantons
Of the East there is no cure. Things
Unconnected seem in harmony, blazon
Before me, the shotgun becomes a decoration
On the wall, and pheasants' wings
Furnish the meadow. Until you turn away
Again negligently, and the reason
Of nature disappears while the universe
Settles into its usual disarray.

1952

RED LANDSCAPE

The red landscape enfolds us,
Autumn exclusive rejects
Frauds, the first snow lacks
Sting but the emptiness proclaims
Retreat and only the boldest
Walk in the face of facts.

No frontier lies between
Us and your hand touches the line
Beyond and draws me into green
Plains rich in summer still;

While mountains of weather lean
All their strength against strange
Intruders, and the country of our love
Puts silence around us, till
Even the wind is only a monotone,
Its echo buried in the hill.

In the following void your words
Are like the thunder of water-falls,
And yet, repeating love, the sweet
Voices of morning birds.

1954

MIDDLE OF THE CENTURY

The sanctity of man propped lone on
The plain edge of winter, not
Day but the dull half white dawn
Of the never-ending snow night,
Is to be thought by us all truly
The projection of our dreams:
We who ran away or failed
To look at the desperate, wholly
Sad and foolish aims
Presented as the natural road
For man and Leviathan: this
Necessary scapegoat's load,
Heart to bear with ordinary eyes
What we avoided, though said
Our facts led to, the emptiness
The prospect before, the fires
Burnt out, the gradual end.

1955

SMALL BOYS PLAYING

The green shadows of small boys,
Playing at soldiers on the village hill,
Round and inchoate like the leaves
In circles on the ground:

Not possible to associate
The sun-light globes between each blade
With oak and mid-day and the sound
Of pulp-mills in the vale.

Too geometric yet too soon
Run the game and saddened gone —
Flag of victory on the hill,
And the shadows massed on the lawn.

1955

A HOUSE IN THE TROPICS

In the early sun the shades are drawn
The streets are empty   the sky a stain
The sails of a ship divide the dawn
The words you said all night remain

The road of morning opens out
All the seasons coincide
The blue of the sea is like a shout
The walls of our love shut in again

The walls of our love shut in again
Time is taken and laid bare
The day assaults us from outside
Like the cold forgotten rain

And like the rain   forgotten   cold
Of another hemisphere
Our memories   nightmares of the soul
Beat on the edges of the year

1958

THE CHILDREN AT CARTAGENA

Under the iron sun
In the arch of day
Seeing the dark children
Happily at play

Some mysterious game
Naive yet intricate
With the years of sorrow
Coming soon or late

Like a thundercloud
In the metal sky
I suddenly recall
Almost totally

Running home from school
Thirty years ago
Slipping on the ice
Sliding on the snow

All my world of love
Dissolved at a touch
I never understood
In that northern dusk

Why what I did was wrong
Or the word absolute
The eye of God blind
The tongue of man mute

So my slender hold
On logic disappeared
And the air was cold
And my tears were real

And the dark children
Wearing masks of joy
Weave circles in the sand
Around that dead boy

1958

EARTHQUAKE

The seasons burn. The wind is dry,
Like the tongue of a sickly dog.
The eyes of the fishermen's wives
Are buried in their dark faces
And the children are all armed with knives.

Nothing in the sensuous street gives
Us warning, even cruelty posted
Everywhere, slinking in the shade,
Or unashamed in the meadows
Of cactus that press upon the dead.

Nothing except love — a warning that
Runs before the earthquake to say
That the streets are opening, the fire
Prepared and the waters of the bay
Ready to resume their empire.

It was in the end a small one, the killed
Very few, the fires soon put out. But not
The memory of the woman running above
The blast with her too late warning
And testimony of love.

1958

THE REFUGEES

The eyes of the refugees are shuttered,
Like the iron windows of the closed shops.
They huddle along the gray walls out of the sun,
And when a lost ray unexpectedly touches them
They look as if they had been thrown
Into the middle of eternity as strangers.

They are only Indians from the high Andes,
Escaping the disaster of some unnamed civil war.
But their mouths hold the same words of pity
As so many others better known. And the gap
Between us is the same, and the distance
Covered, and the hope buried in their faces.

1958

FARTHER LANDSCAPE

There are the mountains
Veiled in obscurity
With a faint snow cap
Shimmering above the hot
Realistic prairies

Hiding a volcano
Perhaps in their
Midst or the legend
Of El Dorado
Or the final death

And here in my hand
Is a fruit ripening
With a strange name
Unpronounceable
A dulcet vowel

Almost as eatable
As the downy skin
On which a drop of water
Forming makes a false
Impression of coolness

And I am almost sure
At that touch that glaze
A cry of memory
Rebounding from the hills
Will break the spell

And start an avalanche
From the improbable
Glacier hidden in the
Tropic peaks into our
Equally improbable vale

1959

71

1960-1969

HURRICANE IN THE CARIBBEAN

A bay left stranded after the flood
On the beach stray dogs   lost cats
Gnawing at the muddy washed-up fish
The waves on the shore ripped by unseen hands

The women pass   dazed   in their eyes
A sudden ray of the immodest sun
The streets full of dead or dying ships
And the harbour with the carcasses of tanks

A soldier guards an unexpected cache
Of gold washed up from the ocean floor
And the crowd that gathers   ragged   dumb
Gaze astonished with a flash of fear

Then rummage in the debris of the port
Or tear strange algae from the roofs
And watch the vultures sailing back
On wings twice as menacing as before

When they all go away and the waves
Reformed depart in Balboa's path
The savage dogs still snuffle on the beach
At the overpowering scent of death

1960

THE RATION OF LOVE

Between night and day lie
The traces of dreams,
Of words carried through the leaves
Of the summer-laden trees.

And through the blurred forest
Of your presence come
The dreams, the words, the promise,
The first murmur of some

Shadow of grace, a lost
Dominion. Spread out
Around us and between us,
Hard to grasp in the rout

Of morning and the stifling mist,
The false purity of isolation
Is stark and ugly in the plain
Of wilderness. As if the ration

Of love had been revealed,
As if the walls had suddenly
Fallen down. Or a crowd
Had invaded the dawn.

And our two worlds — two skies
Reflected in the water.
And the words, spitting dreams,
Needing a century of lies,
Had scarcely an hour to explain.

1960

THE FORBIDDEN GAMES

Outside the geography of time
A round stone, a perfect sphere,
Swings like our planet in an arc,
Swims in space like a tear.

Thrown by a child in a game forbade
The stone distils memory
Of all the games not to be played
In this and every century.

The ball is lost, the child is freed,
All the forbidden games are ours.
But I have forgotten what they mean.
Closed and barred are all the doors.

1960

THE ENGLISH CEMETERY, BOGOTA

It is raining on the English Cemetery
That sudden sullen rain of the tropics
Obscuring the names on the grave-stones
Pushed and elbowed by the great green weeds
And blotting out the Sierra Nevada del Sur
Said to be volcanic

        A bird somewhere
Sings persistently in some protected
Niche and when the voice of the priest
Unexpectedly comes to an end that appears
Definitive all that can be heard is the rain
On the umbrellas and the strangely happy
Voice of the bird

        And if the Sierra Nevada
Should abruptly prove all the pessimists
Right I think the only important fact
That would survive its absolute lava truth
Would be those five sweet notes
Beating a counter-point to the rain.

1961

BOSNIA

Raspolozenje — softly, sweetly the word
Turned on the tongue. She sighed:
Yes, Serbian is a difficult thing —
Like a wild bird, those swallows

There that fly in and out
Of the ruined belfry the Turks
Left as a kind of memento of our
Past — to sting our bandaged eyes.

Raspolozenje — mood, perhaps?
Something like that. The mist
Rising out of the wet snow
Shapes the castle of the Bosnian

Kings into a legend which my books
Deny. It is no more than hearsay,
A starry asterisk, a footnote
To the times — look up dissonance

Of faith, the cynic's price; see
The indifferent turning back
From a problem not our own —
The threshold of our century.

1961

MORNING IN THE DESERT

With the light the sand dunes
Gradually assume shape.
In the night they existed
Almost as a philosophic concept.

Now they shift gently
In the wind, but reduced
To what I can feel and see
In the limits of my horizon.

And the bedouin whose camel
Drifts slowly across the dawn
Sees history in this way.
It is there. It can be seized.
There is nothing irrelevant.

1962

SAKHARA

Here the eye is inevitably cast
Down, fixed on the desert
Floor, staring myopic at the grains
Of sand, until each one
Looks as large and hard as a boulder,
As smooth as a hundred clichés,
All true enough in the sun.

They are like the dogs of the nomads,
Distracting us from the lofty
Contemplation of history. Who cares
Or even hears when the guide
Stumbles through the life story
Of Queen Ti'. We are not overwhelmed
By the palaces and tombs,
Nor burial mounds, nor a majesty
That is as distant as the eyes
Of the bedouin child.
It is a majesty that numbs.

Fascinated rather by the alabaster
Fragments in the rubble of sand
And all the other unimportant
Details that stick in the memory,
While the background of nonsense clings
To the sticky air like thunder
In our own summer country:
The coca-cola vender in the shade,
The tourist camels, the pure
Geometry of Kings.

And one cliché not forgot —
Under the fragile nomad tent,
The half-starved children
In the desert slums.

1963

THE FOUR MONASTERIES OF WADI NATRUN

The white walls are like slabs of salt
Calcinated in the overwhelming sand.
They seem like beads in a chain
Of prayers, a green outbreak of faith

In the desert of unbelief. Calcinated
In the soul and bones, the four saints
Still live, still breathe, still put up
Soft shoots, still water tenderly

The words of God. Behind the reredos
Their eyes, clever under dark unsuspecting
Brows, follow the ritual, in wonderment
That still they live, that still they pray,

That still the word survives —
Desert of four saints.

1963

AVOIDING GREECE

Probably it is the rejection
Of the familiar, as if it were
Unnecessary to investigate
What needs no correction,

The mind being drenched
In the sunlight of stones.
Or can we stand perfection
When it is wrenched

From history? I possibly
Prefer like Cavafy
The half perfect of Alexandria.
It is easier passively

To digest, to absorb slowly
Into one's pores. The trouble is
Can one ever be the same
Again, having thus wholly

Tasted of Greece even there
In Africa. Yet still I go
Round the periphery,
Still hesitate to dare

Lunging into the barren
Truth at the dead centre.

1964

THE GEOMETRY OF WINTER

All the roads are luminous now,
Marked by flags. They stand
Bravely against the black pitch
Of the spruce, like danger signs.

Now there is no fading into the woods.
None can be lost in the bush.
Solitude crowds into solitude
Timorously you take my hand.

The shadows have plunged into
Themselves and there is no
Reflection of us nor movement
Through the winter-robbed underbrush.

The country of innocence is
A mistake of nature. The white
Geometry of winter leaves no margin
For error, no relic in the snow.

The roads, all marked superbly,
Lead as one to the earth's
Centre. Turning back, the paths
Are a black rectangle in the night.

1964

DREAM 64

I am a schizophrenic in the light,
Whole again in the dark,
Early when I should be late,
Know not the face I wear.

I am dismembered, I am ashamed,
Trembling, cold, before
Those grandiloquently doomed
To an outcast life of fear.

Dismemberment — that word I use
To separate the core
Of misery from the decade's rose,
The sick man from the cure.

The hours succeed, the nights destroy,
The world falls fast apart,
And a child sits at the edge of day,
Unconscious of the dark.

Ghost-like we cut our bones away,
And walk with severed heads,
And still hear not the oaths we swear,
Nor contemplate our deeds.

1964

THE SOFT WALLS OF LOVE

From your eyes slowly rises
A lace of mist.
Through its pattern disintegrates
The pleasure that cracks
The arteries of desire.

You too suddenly are vague
And distant.
And behind the mist I see
Black waters with the look
Of invitation to disaster,

Or self-destruction — in our
Days it is all
The same. But spread out as
A night Pacific to my horizon,
Which is not limitless,

Black waters, stippled with
Broken branches
Like the remnants of remorse,
Lap with a long insistency
At the soft walls of love.

1965

THE SHADOW OF YOUR FACE

You are like a door opening on the sky
When I come to the threshold there is no one there

But your shadow is pushed under the mat
And your perfume is in the letter box

The thinnest colour of sunset is in the air
It concentrates the distances from you

A replica of your shadow is in the spaces
That reach like empty words to the dead sky

They are the true sounds of perjury
And they fall like game-birds at my feet

They are the trophies of remorse
Sodden and unrecoverable

They are the burden of the chase
The unacknowledged of defeat

Taking this luggage of the past
I place it near a wall in darkness

And wait unencumbered patiently
For the shadow of your face

1965

INTERRUPTIONS

In the intrusive and insistent sunlight
Of the Delta, made specific by the smell
Of the Nile in flood and the hardly resistant
Shade of the eucalyptus trees,

I think against this sun of all the conquerors
Who faded into the sands, observing
Like Napoleon the curiosities of the land,
Leaving barely a trace on the stone,

Scarce interruptions in the Pharaonic centuries.
The profile of a girl at the well is more
Relevant than control of the Canal,
Than Montgomery and Rommel at Alamein.

Rather — trying to think of history in the village
Café, drinking luke-warm coke, fighting
Flies, but mostly broken into by the memory
Of our short chapter in the chronicles,

I am struck dumb by the camels of the present,
Moving like exalted silhouettes away from
The Delta green, straining, like the Syrian
Monks, toward the deserts of contemplation.

1965

THE VALLEY OF THE RED

The river has overflowed
Its banks and the sand
Bags are spilled and rotted
The water has swelled
Into the ploughed land
Where great lakes
Of snow weighed down with night
Rise to the rains
And the sky comes down to the earth
Like a misshaped hand

The odour of rain and refuse
Has entered my veins
My feet squelch in the mud
And up through the soles
Comes the feel of the underworld
The green wreath
But on the bursting flood
Drifts with a ponderous dignity
The bloated carcass of a horse
And the debris of death

1966

HOW DOTH THE SOLITARY CITY STAND

The lame, the halt, the twisted
And the sick deny
The core of love, their prop in space,
The target missed,

And standing, thwarted and apart,
Silent to praise,
Linger in the emptiness they made,
With melancholy heart.

> Quomodo...sola civitas

Unwhole, the lame brush off
Their tenderness,
And into the solitary city,
Turning again,

Pull down the blinds
On solitary streets.

1966

THE WINTER MEADOWS

The winter meadows   white lagoons of sleep
Have sealed in their heart the memory
Of what we loved and what we were
In the residue of the depths of summer
And in the penetrating deep silence
In the trauma of the north   the fronds
Of pines   frozen in tropic attitudes
Unmoving await a february thaw
Pre-Cambrian details in the green-black woods
They mark the path I would have used
To seek return to what I was

Only the gaps in our experience
The row of empty spaces   the clear
Omissions are the reality
And   like a sacred emptiness
Stretching into the winter steppes
Smother us with their established distances
So that the journey back is no more
Possible than the remembrance
Of an act of love   a show of fear
And the things we did   or think we did
In the landscape of the past

1967

91

1970-1979

WITHOUT HORIZON

We are without horizons.
In the night a cloud of ash
Covered the mirror, the window.

Our dreams have made the sky
The texture of our conscience.
It is very far away.

And when we write in the dust,
On the pane, the message
Is to be read only by ourselves.

1970

WHO WENT BACK

Who went back went in a dream
The road's the same and the gap in the fence
The short-cut through the ravine
And the people haven't changed so much

Who went back never really asked
What leads on beyond that wall
Is there any colour that's really fast
Is there any cure for the common cold

What's the percentage for all of us
The sentiment and the college song
Maybe it isn't there at all
Maybe all of us got it wrong

The footsteps are black in any case
In the early snow which you can see
Is melting fast and beyond the wall
The trees are hushed in the winter maze

What's the angle what's the pitch
Out of the bottom garden gate
Across the meadow and through the ditch
We suddenly come face to face

And recognition is much too late

1971

BEGINNING OF WINTER

The autumn sky has become a litmus
Paper of grey soaking up the earth
While the leaves merge into the mist,
Their colours an obvious lie.

A sparrow fluffs its dull feathers
Shivering on a starkly bare bough.
Its feet seem glued to the damp
Wood. It hardly struggles.

Out of the mist the first flakes of snow
Form solidly from the half rain.
They touch the bird for a moment
Like a crown. Then disappear.

When I look again the bird has somehow
Gone with the snow, perhaps fallen in the
Leaves. It looked impossible it could ever
Fly again. And I do not care

Suddenly if winter is about
To take over the land.

1971

UBIETY

I am in a definite place
At a definite time. And
The geography and the weather
Are of singular unimportance.

Voices, sounds, ideas
Fix a real country, without
Emigration. Its boundaries
Are clear, its mythology known.

The future is laid out flat
Like a mercator's projection.
It has a basis in truth but in fact
Its distortions are predictable.

1972

THE EMIGRANTS

It was not me but someone before me
And maybe someone before that
Who took a ticket on a cattle boat.
Yes, going in the wrong direction.

Out of Rostov-na-Donu, after the pogrom.
The destination didn't matter.
I see them, almost part of me,
Part now of my country.

The last night before a long, long journey,
And it is my journey into the unknown.
They can feel the closeness of the future,
Feel the departure and the homecoming.

There is a smell of death in the odour
Of the lilacs drifting with the wind off the steppe.
And the ticket clenched in one's hand
Is a piece of the holy shroud.

1972

STOPPED IN SPACE

After the frost, before the first
Snow, the water in the pond
Is like baccarat. A bird
On straight sticks of legs

Skates cautiously. Caught in the ice
An autumn leaf, memorialized,
Flashes its still bright vein.
And my eyes are blinded.

The best of us are arrested
In space. We want to sleep
Under the earth but are prisoners
Of the air we so profaned.

1972

THE GRAVE OF PASTERNAK

The wind withers
At the windows of the voices,
Tapping gently, then lost
In the infinite space.
The snow is convent pure.

In the first light
Of Peredelkino
He lies alone with one
Paper flower, faded, wet,
Staining the snow.

The voices can be heard again.
And the windows re-open.

1972

A JOY IN THE AIR

There is a great joy in the air
As the dawn peels off the trees.
The fields become the sea.
The breakers lift away.

The ploughed land under frost
Turns brown suddenly.
The under-brush is astir.
The birds burst into day.

I am almost unaware
Of breathing, so much the sound
Of Spring catches the throat
And logic is a blur.

Perverse I am, persistent
In error, But the world is bright,
There is no sour mirage,
No general disarray.

And so, with fingers crossed,
I put aside my gloom,
Grasp the happy dawn,
And quietly disengage.

1972

THE MESSAGE IS BLURRED

The high tension wires brought
Down in the storm twist in the mud,
Alive like the severed tentacles
Of an octopus, and through

Their throbbing veins lost blood,
Lost energy. The whole neighbourhood
Is dispossessed. Memory
Dispossesses me. Mood

Remains but the thread of thought
Is cut like a spider-web.
No two words are consistent.
Trees are lost for the wood.

And the message I get is blurred
Except for the cypher of your smile.

1973

THE DESERT

After unsleepable nights
The mornings seem insane
From space. Everything

Is taut on the almost
Invisible horizon where
A slight movement betrays it.

Empty. Devoid. No ideas
Come. Meditation only
Over news from nowhere.

1973

THE TUNDRA

The same uninhabited wind,
The same hard drawn sky
As devastates the horizon
Of the Hungry Steppe.

Fine snow like grains of sand,
A tribe of the desert
Which goes out stealthily
To ravage the dawn.

Like bedouin, the wolves
Slip down the skyline,
Just out of sight, waiting
For the first sign of weakness.

1973

INTO THE WILDERNESS

The sun invisible behind the mist
The landscape vague like outer space
Or groping through a world of thought
Alien to the engineers

So many questions to be asked
So many maps that don't exist
What are the sierras in the mind?
Where really does the tree-line run?

By whom in the end are the mountains manned?
What are they armed with in the plain?
And if they are friendly do they know
What love is? Or will they force

Us to shake out our superior brains
And show credentials of a sort?
If love is a valid document
In fact to enter any port

Too many check-points are set up
Too many eyes suspiciously
Peer and probe the absolute
A wilderness as sound as smoke

And silence is the absolute
And the absolute is perfect hate
And in our hands the distances
Softly disintegrate

The landscape blurs the silences
The poles of thought are cancelled out
The expedition never starts
The rim of speculation falls

And in the undecided light
Like a sickly heart the sun
Throbs and swells unevenly
Within the walls of wilderness

1973

THE REVISIONIST

I cannot live without history.
The past is palpable. It is part of me.
I weep for the aborigine
Who at best could remember
Back one generation.

I am sorry for the addict
And the drunkard who close
Out of the past. Even faint
Memories, even twisted and false
Facts, even the artificial myths
Are something to cling to.

History need not be true.
It need only exist.

It strikes deep into emptiness.
It activates the nerves of absence.
It raises the level of tolerance.
It makes me in this poor present
A revisionist of lost days.

1974

WHALE SIGHTING

Barely decypherable, the Via Galactica,
Through the film of mist,
Sheds little light enough
Off the Kamchatka coast.

Enough, enough, to glimpse
A moving black island in the still
Blacker waters — whale!
The curious crowd to the rail,

Ogle the huge back
Before it plunges out of sight.
But how many of the curious ask
How long a respite

Before the murderous factory
Ship arrives, its radar spots
The mighty fins, and
The serious butchery begins.

1974

ANOESIS

In the tight fist of winter
The woods of night slumber.
The snow compresses thought.
I am reduced to dream,
And my dream is congealed in the cold.

February rages, and its last
Rough blundering towards Spring
Blunts the urge to live,
Rationalizes acceptance
Of the slow drift towards death.

This is the danger in our northern world.
Anoesis. We are conscious.
We have sensation. But we
Are dumbed by the world. We accept
Sensation without thought.

1975

HATING POETRY

I am blind with poetry
Sick with the music of it,
Pull tight my carapace
Wad cotton in my ears.

But the arcane syllables
Form like snow flakes in
Frosted air and their noises
Haunt the deaf and dumb.

I am addicted, drugged,
Dragged down by their useless play.
Till one right note from the past
Clears all doubt away.

1975

PIECES OF MEMORY

Little pieces of memory stick
To my skin like broken glass,
The debris of ancient lies,
The webs of old deceits.

Be careful when you pick
Them out not to break open
Some deep vein of remorse.

1975

THE SECOND-RATE

I am picked clean by
        second-rate thoughts.
I cannot chase them away
        like dusty mongrels.
They are the population of our
        epoch
They are the Bolsheviks of our time.

1975

A GANGRENOUS YEAR

Out of the blind gray city,
Beyond the concentric circles of the seasons,
Across the ploughed and heavy land,
The vertiginous song of morning.

Words escape me, or pass me by,
And the subject is avoided.
The morning agony is dissipated
And the year seems tolerable.

The subject is ignored but not
Dropped. It will come up again.
Today the rare winter birds
Are white with astonishment.

But the day is rare and will not
Be repeated. The subject
Cannot be avoided. And the circles
Of the seasons are tightened.

1975

DECEMBER 31, 1974

This year was like a wall before us.
And as it ended what remained
Was bulldozed into brick and
Mortar mixed with dirty slush.

Scratch at the gate of tomorrow,
Promise little. Turn your back
On the long disarray which the
Mind freezes in the marrow.

The cold surf of a song touched
With hoar-frost beats on the window.
Its mute tune turns in the gut,
And my wound burns with my crutch.

So as the sad year ends, this day
Disappears into sullen midnight.
The streets of December long for snow
To cover the year's nudity.

1975

CHANCE

The river is beginning to freeze and
Its waters are dark at the edges
Where the ice is firming. The bridges
Are listening, and the thin landscape
Of the city is still.

So you do not notice the door has
Opened on the somber house, until
That remembered voice invites you in,
And a great solitude comes in with you,
And with the remnants of the day

Denudes your brow of all but the scar
Of memory. In this nakedness the pain
Of another landscape disappears,
And that which awaited our final
Departure, even that which is plain

And familiar, is confounded.
My eclipses are not mathematics,
My returns are not the logical
Syllogism of a well-rounded and thought
Out existence. I am not dependent

On a chain of love, nor the prisoner
Of hope. Only the pattern
Of chance has a claim to validity
In this mechanistic maze.
And in this reasoned jungle I put out

Feelers, only trusting the right
Path will be taken, and not caring
Much if it all turns out to be
In the end a hoax, a fraud,
An endless cul de sac.

1976

THE OTHER SLEEP

For Julien Green

The stain of April is like a star
On the asphalt the puddles
Devastate the last remnants
Of the struggling sun.

I fix the pattern of the rain
Beyond sleep in that second
Stage. It has become
For me the dominant one.

What pins down time in the
Blinding moment is all
Important. In that flash
Of eternity you can see

It must be swept away.
You must return. The future,
Like all tenses, is
Nourished on reality.

Its food is a mixture
Of the possible and
The certain. It is not
The music of childhood

Heard beyond frontiers,
Echoing over the ice-cap.
We fool ourselves in
Reaching for the good.

The sleep-walker must awake.
The evasion must abort.
And the eye take in again
The "real toads" in the mud —

Spattered garden where the rain
Has left its constellations.
Where the hand of April
Is not bathed in blood.

1976

FIRST LOVE

I feel the snow on my face
Like a blind man.

And trace with my fingers
Wet lines of love.

Perhaps I can wipe them away
Without seeing.

1977

A NEW COUNTRY

Now I can talk freely
Because death is in bed with me.
That is the advantage
Of knowing death young.
It has a vast familiarity.
And its visage
Seems somehow homely.

Remember that Spring
When the cherry blossoms won
Against the treacherous frost?
I feel like that to day.
And I see at the bottom
Of your eyes a country
That is new and strange to me.

A land without perimeters,
Without colour, a whole
World of night, a meridian
Of silence, and stopped hours.
Gasping, I break away.
The mirage is gone.

Your face is smiling
Your hand is firm.
There is a mistake somewhere.
The message came up wrong.

1977

118

THE HUBBUB OF APRIL

In the hubbub of April
Long slivers of spring
Creep into the suburbs
And the remains of winter
Break into component parts.

From the organized hills
The melting snow runs
Down all the steep streets
And the tendrils of love
Thrust up through the pavement.

The clangour of time
Bursts out and overwhelms
The lies, walls, webs, the last
Snow flakes, ash, dust, dirt,
The gravel of deceit.

1977

LUNATIC KING

See the blind beggar dance, the cripple sing,
The sot a hero, lunatic a king.

[Alexander Pope]

A snow as thin as lace
Filters the puritan sky,
Floats down hesitantly
On this guilty place.

The time is limpid and its glare
Defies the broken land.
But it cannot hide the smell
Of madness in the air.

The mob in the edgy streets
Is high on LSD.
They welcome the enemy,
Pry wide the prison gates.

The cripples dance, the dumb
Mouth foolish songs of joy.
And the king walks free, victorious,
Wild-eyed, announcing doom.

We, we opened the asylum's doors.
The king is ours by choice.
This is our century.
This is our fatal course.

1977

HOLES IN SPACE

Look, I see holes in space,
And a tenderness
Polished with silence.

A bird singing like an
Organ at vespers
Supplies the counterpoint.

Your eyes become empty
With dreaming
And I can see space between them.

1978

A LATE SPRING

The snotty Spring sniffles
At the threshold, thrusting
Pamphlets and broadsides
Under the door, and when

We open it the snow, again
Falling in sloppy great flakes,
Contradicts you. And the wind
Pushes roughly between

Your legs and the light
Is thinned out and hugged
Against the wall. The garbage
Begins to smell in the thaw,

And I'm sure the river is over
Its banks. Barely visible,
The dawn spreads a stain
Like jealousy, while

The prairies drag against the sky,
Colour of a winter rose,
And you stuff love into a corner
With last week's dirty clothes.

1979

FOR PASTERNAK

I was distracted by the ptarmigan
Whirring up sudden and dusty from
Just in front of me, so did not hear
Your voice saying goodbye.

Goodbye still, in your other voice
Meaning: watch out, time is still.
And goodbye is no worse than a warning
That the months of winter steal.

I am standing with a Russian poet
And I hear him say: "Keep watch,
You must not fall asleep, you are
Eternity's hostage in captivity

To time." And his goodbye means
The captive's hour is coming soon.
But he too looks away at the bird
I thought a ptarmigan, insane

With fear as it flew straight up.
We forget his words of doom
And both look without expectation
For the eggs abandoned in the broom.

1979